V&A
MUSEUM

ARTS AND CRAFTS
ADDRESS BOOK

EBURY PRESS STATIONERY

First published in 1988. This edition published in 1996 by Ebury Press Stationery
an imprint of Random House UK Limited, 20 Vauxhall Bridge Road, London SW1V 2SA

Random House UK Limited Reg. No. 954009

V&A

Set in Garamond by FMT Graphics Ltd., Southwark, London
Printed in Hong Kong
Introduction by Gill Saunders, Department of Designs, Prints and Drawings,
Victoria and Albert Museum.
Picture research by Gill Saunders and Hilary Young
Inside designed by Polly Dawes
Cover designed by David Fordham

ISBN 0 7126 2443 0

Front cover illustration: 'Hare'. Detail from 'The Forest' tapestry, 1887. The tapestry was designed by William Morris
(1834-96), but the animals are after drawings by Philip Webb – a founder member of Morris' firm – and the foreground
details were designed by Henry Dearle.

Back cover illustration: 'The Strawberry Thief' (*detail*), printed cotton by William Morris, Morris & Co., 1883.

Introduction illustration: Robert Percy Gossop. Decorative envelope with caricature of the textile and
wallpaper designer Lindsay P. Butterfield, watercolour and Indian ink, 1901. Little is known about the
artist other than that he worked as a magazine illustrator, and that he was active between 1901 and 1925.

THE
ARTS AND CRAFTS
MOVEMENT

he guiding principle of the Arts and Crafts movement was a desire to improve standards of design in the decorative and domestic arts by a revival of handcrafts, 'the true root and basis of all Art' according to designer and propagandist Walter Crane (1845–1915). The rise of the movement was part of the reaction against what were seen as the ugly mass-produced wares predominant in the displays at the Great Exhibition of 1851. The critic John Ruskin had identified urbanisation and mechanisation as the underlying causes of a moral degeneration in art and society. His disciple William Morris (1834–96), who was to dominate Arts and Crafts both in theory and in practice, developed these ideas into an idealistic political creed which in turn informed his artistic production.

Attempts to furnish his first home in London, and later the Red House, built for him by Philip Webb (1831–1915) in 1860, revealed to Morris that 'all the minor arts were in a state of complete degradation'. His response was the foundation of Morris, Marshall, Faulkner & Co. to produce embroideries, wallpapers, tiles, stained glass, woven and printed textiles, carpets, metalwork and furniture. Crane later described the work of the Morris firm as 'in the main a revival of the medieval spirit (not the letter) in design; a return to simplicity, to sincerity; to good materials and sound workmanship; to rich and suggestive surface decoration and simple conservative forms . . .'.

Arts and Crafts ornament was characterised by a romanticised medievalism and the evidence of a direct study of natural forms. As Morris said, 'And for your teachers, let them be nature and history'. He himself studied exhaustively at the Victoria and Albert Museum, using the collections perhaps 'more than any man living'. This sense of history included a new respect for traditional and vernacular forms in English craft and architecture. The Red House embodies the Arts and Crafts ideal; described by Morris as being 'in the style of the 13th century' it unites truth to materials with fitness for purpose.

Morris' romantic socialism was manifested in a desire to create art for all (a purpose ultimately defeated by his insistence on costly handcraft processes) and fostered a cooperative spirit in Arts and Crafts practice. Hence the establishment of guilds on the medieval model, by A.H. Mackmurdo (1882), C.R. Ashbee (1888) and others. The essential aim was to reunite the functions of artist and craftsman, a practice abandoned in the Renaissance and seen as the fundamental cause of degeneration in the decorative arts.

The Victoria and Albert Museum itself (established in 1857) grew out of Arts and Crafts principles, offering examples of good design to inspire designers and manufacturers. Arts and Crafts material is strongly represented in the collections in all media. The Museum began to buy work from Morris as early as 1864, the first purchase being four panels of stained glass, and the following year commissioned the decoration of what became known as the Green Dining Room. This scheme is typical of the movement's earliest style with rich but sombre colour, extensive use of simple flat pattern and an abundance of medieval motifs. In time, Arts and Crafts design, in the hands of Mackmurdo, Crane and C.F.A. Voysey, became lighter and more sophisticated, prefiguring Art Nouveau.

Gill Saunders
Department of Designs, Prints & Drawings

The Victoria and Albert Museum

The Victoria and Albert Museum is Britain's national museum of art and design. The Museum's enormous collections trace the history of the decorative arts from early Christian times to the present, not only from Europe but also from China, India, Japan and the world of Islam.

ngeli Laudantes. Tapestry, woven in 1894 at Morris & Co.'s Merton Abbey Tapestry works. The composition is taken from a Burne-Jones design of 1878 for a stained glass window for Salisbury Cathedral. 'Angeli Laudantes' can be translated as 'Angels Offering Praise'.

· angeli · laudantes ·

Name

Address

Phone

Name

Address

Phone

Name

Address

Phone

Name

Address

Phone

Name

Address

Phone

Name

Address

Phone

Name

Address

Phone

Name

Address

Phone

Name

Address

Phone

Name

Address

Phone

Name

Address

Phone

Name

Address

Phone

Name

Address

Phone

Name

Address

Phone

Name

Address

Phone

Name

Address

Phone

Name

Address

Phone

Name

Address

Phone

Name

Address

Phone

Name

Address

Phone

Name

Address

Phone

urne-Jones, Sir Edward Coley, Bart (1838–98). 'Merlin and Nimue', watercolour, 1861. Painted at a time when the artist was very much influenced by Rossetti. The subject is taken from Sir Thomas Malory's 'Le Morte d'Arthur', but Burne-Jones has departed from Malory's account in several respects.

Name

Address

Phone

Name

Address

Phone

Name

Address

Phone

Name

Address

Phone

Name

Address

Phone

Name

Address

Phone

Name

Address

Phone

Name

Address

Phone

Name

Address

Phone

Name

Address

Phone

Name

Address

Phone

Name

Address

Phone

Name

Address

Phone

Name

Address

Phone

Name

Address

Phone

Name

Address

Phone

Name

Address

Phone

Name

Address

Phone

Name

Address

Phone

Name

Address

Phone

Name

Address

Phone

haucer Asleep. Stained glass panel made by Morris, Marshall, Faulkner & Co., c.1860. Chaucer was an obvious hero for the Arts and Crafts movement; one of the first publications from Morris' Kelmscott Press was an edition of his works designed in imitation of medieval illuminated manuscripts.

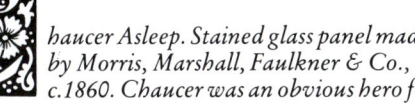

Name

Address

Phone

Name

Address

Phone

Name

Address

Phone

Name

Address

Phone

Name

Address

Phone

Name

Address

Phone

Name

Address

Phone

Name

Address

Phone

Name

Address

Phone

Name

Address

Phone

Name

Address

Phone

Name

Address

Phone

Name

Address

Phone

Name

Address

Phone

Name

Address

Phone

Name

Address

Phone

Name

Address

Phone

Name

Address

Phone

Name

Address

Phone

Name

Address

Phone

Name

Address

Phone

ream of John Ball. Written by William
Morris (1834–96), illustrated by
Edward Burne-Jones (1833–98), 1892.
A plate from one of the elaborate illustrated books produced by
Morris at the Kelmscott Press. The woodcut medium was favoured
for its obvious hand-crafted quality.

WHEN ADAM DELVED
AND EVE SPAN
WHO WAS THEN THE
GENTLEMAN

Name

Address

Phone

Name

Address

Phone

Name

Address

Phone

Name

Address

Phone

Name

Address

Phone

Name

Address

Phone

Name

Address

Phone

Name

Address

Phone

Name

Address

Phone

Name

Address

Phone

Name

Address

Phone

Name

Address

Phone

Name

Address

Phone

Name

Address

Phone

Name

Address

Phone

Name

Address

Phone

Name

Address

Phone

Name

Address

Phone

Name

Address

Phone

Name

Address

Phone

Name

Address

Phone

*mbroidered hanging. 'The Artichoke',
crewel-work on linen, 1877. Designed
by William Morris (1834–96). One of three
known embroideries worked to this design by Mrs Ada Phoebe
Godman for her home, Smeaton Manor, near Northallerton.*

Name

Address

Phone

Name

Address

Phone

Name

Address

Phone

Name

Address

Phone

Name

Address

Phone

Name

Address

Phone

Name

Address

Phone

Name

Address

Phone

Name

Address

Phone

Name

Address

Phone

Name

Address

Phone

Name

Address

Phone

Name

Address

Phone

Name

Address

Phone

Name

Address

Phone

Name

Address

Phone

Name

Address

Phone

Name

Address

Phone

Name

Address

Phone

Name

Address

Phone

Name

Address

Phone

our tiles by William de Morgan (1839–1917), tin-glazed earthenware. De Morgan drew much of his inspiration from Persian ceramics, favouring oriental forms and rich glowing colour.

Name

Address

Phone

Name

Address

Phone

Name

Address

Phone

Name

Address

Phone

Name

Address

Phone

Name

Address

Phone

Name

Address

Phone

Name

Address

Phone

Name

Address

Phone

Name

Address

Phone

Name

Address

Phone

Name

Address

Phone

Name

Address

Phone

Name

Address

Phone

Name

Address

Phone

Name

Address

Phone

Name

Address

Phone

Name

Address

Phone

Name

Address

Phone

Name

Address

Phone

Name

Address

Phone

reen Dining Room, Victoria and Albert
Museum. Original design for gesso
panelling and painted plaster frieze by
Philip Webb (1831–1915), watercolour, 1866. This was the first
commission for a complete decorative scheme to be undertaken by
Morris & Co., and is the only Morris interior to have survived intact.

Name

Address

Phone

Name

Address

Phone

Name

Address

Phone

Name

Address

Phone

Name

Address

Phone

Name

Address

Phone

Name

Address

Phone

Name

Address

Phone

Name

Address

Phone

Name

Address

Phone

Name

Address

Phone

Name

Address

Phone

Name

Address

Phone

Name

Address

Phone

Name

Address

Phone

Name

Address

Phone

Name

Address

Phone

Name

Address

Phone

Name

Address

Phone

Name

Address

Phone

Name

Address

Phone

*are. Detail from 'The Forest' tapestry,
1887. The tapestry was designed by
William Morris (1834–96), but the animals
are after drawings by Philip Webb – a founder member of Morris'
firm – and the foreground details were designed by Henry Dearle.*

Name

Address

Phone

Name

Address

Phone

Name

Address

Phone

Name

Address

Phone

Name

Address

Phone

Name

Address

Phone

Name

Address

Phone

Name

Address

Phone

Name

Address

Phone

Name

Address

Phone

Name

Address

Phone

Name

Address

Phone

Name

Address

Phone

Name

Address

Phone

Name

Address

Phone

Name

Address

Phone

Name

Address

Phone

Name

Address

Phone

Name

Address

Phone

Name

Address

Phone

Name

Address

Phone

*sis. Design for a wallpaper frieze by C. F. A. Voysey (1857–1941), watercolour, c. 1893. Initially influenced by Morris, Voysey developed a personal style of greater lightness and elegance. His most typical patterns feature large areas of flat, clear colour.*

Name

Address

Phone

Name

Address

Phone

Name

Address

Phone

Name

Address

Phone

Name

Address

Phone

Name

Address

Phone

Name

Address

Phone

Name _____

Address _____

_____

Phone _____

Name _____

Address _____

_____

Phone _____

Name _____

Address _____

_____

Phone _____

Name _____

Address _____

_____

Phone _____

Name _____

Address _____

_____

Phone _____

Name _____

Address _____

_____

Phone _____

Name _____

Address _____

_____

Phone _____

Name

Address

Phone

Name

Address

Phone

Name

Address

Phone

Name

Address

Phone

Name

Address

Phone

Name

Address

Phone

Name

Address

Phone

asmine. Wallpaper by William Morris (1834–96), colour print from wood blocks, 1872. Morris' later designs are characterised by a vigorous and complex rhythmic structure that effectively disguises the pattern repeat.

J

Name

Address

Phone

Name

Address

Phone

Name

Address

Phone

Name

Address

Phone

Name

Address

Phone

Name

Address

Phone

Name

Address

Phone

Name

Address

Phone

Name

Address

Phone

Name

Address

Phone

Name

Address

Phone

Name

Address

Phone

Name

Address

Phone

Name

Address

Phone

Name

Address

Phone

Name

Address

Phone

Name

Address

Phone

Name

Address

Phone

Name

Address

Phone

Name

Address

Phone

Name

Address

Phone

ing Rene's Honeymoon. Stained glass panel from a series designed by D. G. Rossetti (1828–82) and made by Morris, Marshall, Faulkner & Co., 1862. A typical example of the medieval taste which the Arts and Crafts movement shared with the Pre-Raphaelite painters, this scene is an imaginary incident from the story of King Rene of Anjou as recounted in Sir Walter Scott's 'Anna von Geierstein.'

Name

Address

Phone

Name

Address

Phone

Name

Address

Phone

Name

Address

Phone

Name

Address

Phone

Name

Address

Phone

Name

Address

Phone

Name

Address

Phone

Name

Address

Phone

Name

Address

Phone

Name

Address

Phone

Name

Address

Phone

Name

Address

Phone

Name

Address

Phone

Name

Address

Phone

Name

Address

Phone

Name

Address

Phone

Name

Address

Phone

Name

Address

Phone

Name

Address

Phone

Name

Address

Phone

et Us Prey. Undated design by C. F. A. Voysey (1857–1941) for a printed furnishing fabric, watercolour. The design is based on the motif of a cat watching a canary, which in turn preys on a worm. Though he always signed himself 'C. F. A. Voysey, Architect', flat pattern design formed a major part of Voysey's work throughout his career.

L

Name

Address

Phone

Name

Address

Phone

Name

Address

Phone

Name

Address

Phone

Name

Address

Phone

Name

Address

Phone

Name

Address

Phone

Name

Address

Phone

Name

Address

Phone

Name

Address

Phone

Name

Address

Phone

Name

Address

Phone

Name

Address

Phone

Name

Address

Phone

Name

Address

Phone

Name

Address

Phone

Name

Address

Phone

Name

Address

Phone

Name

Address

Phone

Name

Address

Phone

Name

Address

Phone

orris, William (1834–96). 'Rose',
wallpaper, colour print from wood
blocks, 1877. Morris' wallpaper designs
became increasingly dense and sophisticated, without losing the
restraint and order which distinguished his work from the
overblown naturalism of contemporary machine-printed papers.

Name

Address

Phone

Name

Address

Phone

Name

Address

Phone

Name

Address

Phone

Name

Address

Phone

Name

Address

Phone

Name

Address

Phone

Name

Address

Phone

Name

Address

Phone

Name

Address

Phone

Name

Address

Phone

Name

Address

Phone

Name

Address

Phone

Name

Address

Phone

Name

Address

Phone

Name

Address

Phone

Name

Address

Phone

Name

Address

Phone

Name

Address

Phone

Name

Address

Phone

Name

Address

Phone

 apper, Harry (d.1930). 'Teazle', design
for a printed fabric, watercolour, 1899-
1900. The design was produced as a
block-printed velveteen by G. P. & J. Baker Ltd. Harry Napper
was a designer of repeating patterns, metalwork and furniture,
and a watercolour artist. He worked for the Silver Studio, a design
agency, from 1893 to 1903.

Name

Address

Phone

Name

Address

Phone

Name

Address

Phone

Name

Address

Phone

Name

Address

Phone

Name

Address

Phone

Name

Address

Phone

Name

Address

Phone

Name

Address

Phone

Name

Address

Phone

Name

Address

Phone

Name

Address

Phone

Name

Address

Phone

Name

Address

Phone

Name

Address

Phone

Name

Address

Phone

Name

Address

Phone

Name

Address

Phone

Name

Address

Phone

Name

Address

Phone

ak silk damask embroidered as a
portière by Mrs Battye, after a design by
Henry Dearle, c.1890 (detail). Dearle
(1860–1932) worked for William Morris from 1878. He designed
many of Morris & Co.'s textiles and wallpapers from the late
1880s, and, on Morris' death, in 1896, he became the Art Director
of the firm.

O

Name

Address

Phone

Name

Address

Phone

Name

Address

Phone

Name

Address

Phone

Name

Address

Phone

Name

Address

Phone

Name

Address

Phone

Name

Address

Phone

Name

Address

Phone

Name

Address

Phone

Name

Address

Phone

Name

Address

Phone

Name

Address

Phone

Name

Address

Phone

Name

Address

Phone

Name

Address

Phone

Name

Address

Phone

Name

Address

Phone

Name

Address

Phone

Name

Address

Phone

Name

Address

Phone

eacock sconce. Steel, bronze, brass and silver with enamelled decoration. Designed and made by Alexander Fisher (1864–1936), and exhibited at the Arts and Crafts Exhibition in 1899. Fisher's enamelled pieces were highly influential on the work of British art-metalworkers in the years around 1900.

Name

Address

Phone

Name

Address

Phone

Name

Address

Phone

Name

Address

Phone

Name

Address

Phone

Name

Address

Phone

Name

Address

Phone

Name

Address

Phone

Name

Address

Phone

Name

Address

Phone

Name

Address

Phone

Name

Address

Phone

Name

Address

Phone

Name

Address

Phone

Name

Address

Phone

Name

Address

Phone

Name

Address

Phone

Name

Address

Phone

Name

Address

Phone

Name

Address

Phone

Name

Address

Phone

ueen of Hearts. Detail from 'Alice in Wonderland', a design by C. F. A. Voysey (1857–1941) for a furnishing fabric, watercolour on photostatic print, 1930. Produced as a glazed chintz by Morton Sundour Fabrics. The same figures, taken from Sir John Tenniel's illustrations to the Alice books, also appear on transfer-printed tiles designed by Voysey.

Q

Name

Address

Phone

Name

Address

Phone

Name

Address

Phone

Name

Address

Phone

Name

Address

Phone

Name

Address

Phone

Name

Address

Phone

Name

Address

Phone

Name

Address

Phone

Name

Address

Phone

Name

Address

Phone

Name

Address

Phone

Name

Address

Phone

Name

Address

Phone

Name

Address

Phone

Name

Address

Phone

Name

Address

Phone

Name

Address

Phone

Name

Address

Phone

Name

Address

Phone

Name

Address

Phone

*ose. Printed furnishing fabric. Designed by William Morris (1834–96) (the design registered 1883), and indigo discharge-printed at Merton Abbey. Like many of Morris' designs for printed and woven textiles, 'Rose' is derived from the compartmentalised 'pomegranate' patterns of 15th and 16th century Italian silks and velvets.*

R

Name

Address

Phone

Name

Address

Phone

Name

Address

Phone

Name

Address

Phone

Name

Address

Phone

Name

Address

Phone

Name

Address

Phone

Name

Address

Phone

Name

Address

Phone

Name

Address

Phone

Name

Address

Phone

Name

Address

Phone

Name

Address

Phone

Name

Address

Phone

Name

Address

Phone

Name

Address

Phone

Name

Address

Phone

Name

Address

Phone

Name

Address

Phone

Name

Address

Phone

Name

Address

Phone

*ir Lancelot. Panel of stained and painted
glass designed by Edward Burne-Jones
(1833–98) and made by Morris & Co.,
c.1880–90. The linear style and rich colour of Burne-Jones'
paintings translated very successfully into the medium of stained glass.*

S

Name

Address

Phone

Name

Address

Phone

Name

Address

Phone

Name

Address

Phone

Name

Address

Phone

Name

Address

Phone

Name

Address

Phone

Name

Address

Phone

Name

Address

Phone

Name

Address

Phone

Name

Address

Phone

Name

Address

Phone

Name

Address

Phone

Name

Address

Phone

Name

Address

Phone

Name

Address

Phone

Name

Address

Phone

Name

Address

Phone

Name

Address

Phone

Name

Address

Phone

Name

Address

Phone

rellis. Wallpaper by William Morris (1834–96), colour print from wood blocks, 1864. This was the first wallpaper Morris designed, intended for the Red House and inspired by its gardens. It has the vigorous naivety which characterised much early Arts and Crafts material.

T

Name

Address

Phone

Name

Address

Phone

Name

Address

Phone

Name

Address

Phone

Name

Address

Phone

Name

Address

Phone

Name

Address

Phone

Name

Address

Phone

Name

Address

Phone

Name

Address

Phone

Name

Address

Phone

Name

Address

Phone

Name

Address

Phone

Name

Address

Phone

Name

Address

Phone

Name

Address

Phone

Name

Address

Phone

Name

Address

Phone

Name

Address

Phone

Name

Address

Phone

Name

Address

Phone

ntitled block-printed linen, 1903. Designed by Lindsay P. Butterfield (1869–1948), printed by G. P. & J. Baker Ltd, and sold through Liberty & Co. Butterfield was a prolific pattern designer who supplied drawings to many of the leading textile manufacturers, Alexander Morton, Turnbull & Stockdale, and Warner's, among them.

U

Name

Address

Phone

Name

Address

Phone

Name

Address

Phone

Name

Address

Phone

Name

Address

Phone

Name

Address

Phone

Name

Address

Phone

Name

Address

Phone

Name

Address

Phone

Name

Address

Phone

Name

Address

Phone

Name

Address

Phone

Name

Address

Phone

Name

Address

Phone

Name

Address

Phone

Name

Address

Phone

Name

Address

Phone

Name

Address

Phone

Name

Address

Phone

Name

Address

Phone

Name

Address

Phone

oysey, Charles Francis Annesley (1857–1941). 'The Wykehamist', detail from a machine-woven Axminster carpet made by Tomkinson and Adam, 1897. Like many of Voysey's repeating patterns, this design was produced in a number of media, in this case also as a wallpaper and woven fabric.

Name

Address

Phone

Name

Address

Phone

Name

Address

Phone

Name

Address

Phone

Name

Address

Phone

Name

Address

Phone

Name

Address

Phone

Name

Address

Phone

Name

Address

Phone

Name

Address

Phone

Name

Address

Phone

Name

Address

Phone

Name

Address

Phone

Name

Address

Phone

Name

Address

Phone

Name

Address

Phone

Name

Address

Phone

Name

Address

Phone

Name

Address

Phone

Name

Address

Phone

Name

Address

Phone

oman playing the lute. Panel of stained and painted glass designed by William Morris (1834–96), c.1872–4. True to his principles, Morris was actively involved in all aspects of his firm's output. Though primarily a designer, he also learned a variety of craft techniques, from painting and carving to dyeing and weaving.

Name

Address

Phone

Name

Address

Phone

Name

Address

Phone

Name

Address

Phone

Name

Address

Phone

Name

Address

Phone

Name

Address

Phone

Name

Address

Phone

Name

Address

Phone

Name

Address

Phone

Name

Address

Phone

Name

Address

Phone

Name

Address

Phone

Name

Address

Phone

Name

Address

Phone

Name

Address

Phone

Name

Address

Phone

Name

Address

Phone

Name

Address

Phone

Name

Address

Phone

Name

Address

Phone

acht attacked by a sea monster. Design by William de Morgan (1839–1917) for a lustre painted earthenware dish, bodycolour, pricked for transfer, 1879. The Islamic technique of decorating pottery with ruby lustre glazes was revived by de Morgan in the 1870s. He had re-discovered the technique while working as a stained glass artist during the previous decade.

Name

Address

Phone

Name

Address

Phone

Name

Address

Phone

Name

Address

Phone

Name

Address

Phone

Name

Address

Phone

Name

Address

Phone

Name

Address

Phone

Name

Address

Phone

Name

Address

Phone

Name

Address

Phone

Name

Address

Phone

Name

Address

Phone

Name

Address

Phone

Name

Address

Phone

Name

Address

Phone

Name

Address

Phone

Name

Address

Phone

Name

Address

Phone

Name

Address

Phone

Name

Address

Phone